STEPS TO LAUNCHING YOUR OWN BUSINESS: A BEGINNER'S GUIDE

Virginia Marc

STEPS TO LAUNCHING YOUR OWN BUSINESS: A BEGINNER'S GUIDE

Copyright © 2021 Virginia Marc

All rights reserved

ISBN.13: 978-0-578-89166-8

VIRGINIA MARC

CONTENTS

ACKNOWLEDGMENTS **3**

INTRODUCTION **4**

CHAPTER 1: FIND YOUR NICHE **9**

CHAPTER 2: CHOOSING THE RIGHT BUSINESS ENTITY **13**

CHAPTER 3: REGISTER YOUR BUSINESS' NAME **35**

CHAPTER 4: CREATING A BUSINESS PLAN **44**

CHAPTER 5: SOCIAL MEDIA **48**

CHAPTER 6: AUTOMATE YOUR BUSINESS **62**

CHAPTER 7: CHOOSING & PRICING YOUR PRODUCT/SERVICE **74**

CHAPTER 8: READY! SET! LAUNCH! **103**

STEPS TO LAUNCHING YOUR OWN BUSINESS: A BEGINNER'S GUIDE

ACKNOWLEDGEMENTS

Special thank you to the Creator of the Universe for putting this idea into my heart. Thank you to those individuals who reached out to me with questions how to start a business as you are the inspiration behind this project.

VIRGINIA MARC

INTRODUCTION

If you are reading this, you have made your mind up that working a nine to five just is not for you and you are ready to branch out into entrepreneurship. But you are unsure of where or even how to get started with building a business of your own. I know this because I too was once in your shoes. I had no clue as to what needed to be done first. I had no product or service to sell. I took a step back and realized I had to do my homework. It took some research as well as trial and error. I failed a few times before I could get it right. Therefore, my goal with this step-by-step guide is to help you achieve an easy transition into entrepreneurship. I encourage you to keep this guide close as you embark on your new journey to becoming the fearless boss you were meant to be.

Please allow me to tell you about my background. I graduated from Florida Agricultural and Mechanical University with a Bachelor of Science in Biology. I did not graduate with honors, and I accumulated thousands of dollars of debt in student loans. From there I had dreams of becoming a Dentist which would have required another four years of study. However,

STEPS TO LAUNCHING YOUR OWN BUSINESS: A BEGINNER'S GUIDE

this would have required I complete and pass the DAT, but it is safe to say that test-taking just was not my thing. My dream of becoming a Dentist became non-existent. Listening to family and friends who suggested I continue my education, I enrolled in a graduate program at Life University. After completing two years of study, I had maxed out on my student loan allowance and could no longer afford tuition which in turn I ended up dropping the program. Shortly after I moved back home with my parents and was working as a telemarketer to help pay back student loans. Since I already had background in science and experience in the dental field from my days back in high school, I decided to complete a Dental Assisting certificate program at Sanford Brown Institute. It allowed me to earn a decent living to help pay down my student loan debt. I worked as a dental assistant for eighteen years before I realized I had lost my zeal for the industry. Even though this industry was quite rewarding, this was not the plan I had for my life. I did not complete six years of college for me to end

VIRGINIA MARC

up being someone's assistant for the rest of my life. In fact, I always had dreams of becoming my own boss, just had no idea how to make that happen. I then found myself wishing I had majored in business or finance. However, I had wasted too many years of my life to continue living in resentment. I had become paralyzed by fear of failure and was doubting myself. I could no longer let fear control my life and knew I had to do something about it. When life pushes you to the limit you are faced with the decision to stay stagnant or do something to change your situation. I chose the latter of the two. I knew it was time for me boss up but if I was going to do it, I had to do so fearlessly.

I began to embark on the journey of entrepreneurship. I remember being introduced to network marketing and affiliate marketing sometime in twenty-ten. For those who are not familiar with network marketing also known as multi-level marketing it follows a business model that depends on person-to-person sales usually featuring a low upfront investment and includes building a network of business partners to assist with lead generation to sell a product or service. Affiliate marketing is a performance-

STEPS TO LAUNCHING YOUR OWN BUSINESS: A BEGINNER'S GUIDE

based marketing in which a business rewards an affiliate with a commission for referring the business's product or service. To become an affiliate marketer there is no startup cost. Both are great do not get me wrong, however, the keyword in network marketing is "network" which is defined as a group or system of interconnected people or things. This line of business requires being connected to a lot of people. There usually was one top earner in the company while it seemed as though others on the bottom of the pyramid struggled with making even one sale. Long story short I had tried my hand in this industry and saw success but nothing extravagant. It took me another ten years to figure out that I was still working to make someone else rich, and I was ready to be the founder and CEO of my own company. It is safe to assume that you too are seeking business ownership, which is what brought you to this guide. I encourage you to continue reading this guide so you can learn the steps you need to take now to get you going in the right direction.

VIRGINIA MARC

This beginner's guide was created to answer those critical questions when deciding to go into business for yourself. It provides excellent resources to save time and avoid you having to go searching it all on your own. I must give you the disclaimer that I do not provide legal, or tax advice and this article is not a substitute for advice from an attorney or tax advisor. It is encouraged that you still do your own research and seek the help of a professional where needed. In this guide I provide the information I wish someone had given me when I first decided to go into business. I hope you find this guide to be a helpful resource.

STEPS TO LAUNCHING YOUR OWN BUSINESS: A BEGINNER'S GUIDE

CHAPTER 1: FIND YOUR NICHE

So, you have made the conscious decision to become a founder and CEO of your very own company, but you do not have a product or service to sell. Well news flash, entrepreneurship begins well before business ownership. It begins with personal ownership of yourself and your career. It is important to understand that entrepreneurship is a mindset and we as individuals are responsible for our own happiness and self-fulfillment. If you need help trying to find your niche this chapter is for you. However, if you already have your niche feel free to skip ahead to the next chapter. Also, choosing and pricing your product will be discussed in greater detail in chapter 7. In this chapter the idea is to get your creative juices flowing if you have not figured out what product or service you plan to offer.

In case you are wondering what a "niche" is, it is a specialized segment of the market for a particular kind of product or service. Finding your niche should start with you asking yourself these important questions: What is it

VIRGINIA MARC

that you want to share with others? How is my product and/or service going to help others? Does my product and/or service provide consumers with a solution to a problem? Take this example into consideration. You are wanting to start a YouTube channel center focus on skincare. This is broad but narrow it down maybe to a specific audience. Say for example your audience is looking for help with getting rid of dark spots due to hyperpigmentation. You would want to create a video that focuses on "how to get rid of dark spots caused by scarring from acne and hyperpigmentation?" This now answers your audience's question and provides a solution to their problem. Do not be concerned with creating a niche that others are already monetizing from. Just because it was already done does not mean you cannot make your own mark in the same industry. Do not believe me, think about big brands like Coca-Cola (Coke) and Pepsi. Some may argue Coca-Cola is better than Pepsi even though in my opinion they both taste the same. But you have some individuals who are team Pepsi and some who are team Coke. Even though they are so much a like they both managed to make their mark in the beverage industry and made a

STEPS TO LAUNCHING YOUR OWN BUSINESS: A BEGINNER'S GUIDE

huge name for themselves. Are you still doubting yourself? You want to create a swimwear line, but we all know there are so many others out there. Here is what you do, scope out the competition study what they are doing and produce a way to put your own spin on it. You might take notice that your competition is offering an incentive giving its consumers ten percent off when they spend forty dollars, so you can up the ante and offer fifteen percent off. You could also offer a rewards program for loyal customers allowing them to redeem rewards for free swimwear or get a discount on purchases.

Finding a niche might be difficult but take a moment if you do not have a niche to write down ideas that come to mind. Think about what you hope to accomplish with your product or service. Find purpose! Once you can find purpose in your work, you unlock the highest level of motivation. Think about the happiest people in the world and you will recognize that their passion is linked to a deep sense of purpose whether they are providing

VIRGINIA MARC

a recreation center for children or working towards the best customer experiences possible. In addition to the questions mentioned previously, ask yourself:

- What is the big picture and how is what I am doing connected to some higher purpose?
- Is my work making a social impact?

Successful founders/owners have figured out the importance of these elements and have taken personal ownership by making the effort to create a life where autonomy, knowledge and purpose can thrive. Remember entrepreneurship is about taking real ownership of yourself and your career by challenging yourself to think big and get motivated.

STEPS TO LAUNCHING YOUR OWN BUSINESS: A BEGINNER'S GUIDE

CHAPTER 2: CHOOSING THE RIGHT BUSINESS ENTITY

You have made the conscious decision to go into business for yourself and have produced a niche (a specialized segment of the market for a particular kind of product or service) and decided what you want to name your business. When registering your business take into consideration the type of operation you are starting, how big it is, and what state you live in. I will explain the basics of how to get your business registered, however, I do not provide legal, nor tax advice and this writing is not a substitute for advice from an attorney or tax advisor.

When going into business for yourself, one of the most important decisions you will make is, which legal form your business will take. The legal form or business entity you choose will affect the way you file for taxes, whether you will be liable for your business's debts, and how the IRS and state auditors will treat you.

VIRGINIA MARC

The following are four major business entities that will be discussed in this chapter:

- Sole proprietorship
- Corporation
    - C-Corporation
    - S-Corporation
- Partnership
- Limited liability corporation

Keep in mind, if you own your business alone, partnerships will not apply to you because this business entity requires two or more owners. Even if you are unsure of which business form to choose now, you can always switch to a different legal form later. According to Stephen Fishman, J.D., author of "Working for Yourself: Law & Taxes for Independent Contractors, Freelancers, & Consultants," it is common for self-employed people to start out as sole proprietors, then incorporate or form limited liability corporations (LLCs) later when they become better established and make a

STEPS TO LAUNCHING YOUR OWN BUSINESS: A BEGINNER'S GUIDE

substantial amount of income. The remainder of this chapter will explain each of these entities in more detail.

Sole Proprietorships

A sole proprietorship is exactly what it indicates, there is only one business owner. A major advantage to this legal form is that it is the most affordable and easiest legal form for organizing your business. Permission from the government is not required nor are you required to pay any fees, except for a fictious business name or business license. If you are already running a one-person business and never select a business structure, then you categorize as a sole proprietorship. This entity makes up majority of self-employed individuals. According to a recent survey, seventy-three percent of all businesses in the U.S. are sole proprietor businesses. Most sole proprietors run small operations but can also hire employees and other contractors too. If you are already running a one-person business (or considering starting one), the sole proprietorship form is an excellent choice. However, do keep in mind your business and personal assets and liabilities are not separate. You do not pay taxes or file tax returns separately for your sole proprietorship. Instead, you must report the income you earn or losses you incur on your own personal tax return, IRS Form 1040.

EXAMPLE: John operates an online business consulting firm as a sole proprietor. He must report all the income he receives from his clients on his individual tax return, IRS Form 1040, and file Schedule C. He does not need to file a separate tax return for his business. In the recent year, he earned seventy-five thousand dollars from consulting but incurred ten thousand dollars in business expenses, leaving a net business income of sixty-five thousand dollars. He reports his gross profits from consulting and his business expenses on Schedule C. He must add his sixty-five-thousand-dollar profit to any other income he has and reports the total on his form 1040. He must pay both income tax and self-employment tax on this profit. With every advantage usually there are disadvantages.

As a sole proprietor you are liable for all the debts of your business meaning a creditor can go after all your business and personal assets.

STEPS TO LAUNCHING YOUR OWN BUSINESS: A BEGINNER'S GUIDE

Concisely your personal or business bank accounts, equipment, your car, and even your house can all be targeted. You will also be personally liable for business-related liability lawsuits such as premises, infringement, employer, product, or negligence. Another disadvantage of being a sole proprietor is that in the eyes of the IRS or auditors it does not help you establish business ownership. Sole proprietors who provide services can look like employees, especially if their deposits are made in a personal bank account. Let us move on to the next entity I want to discuss.

Corporations

So, what is a corporation? Investopedia defines corporation as a legal entity that is separate and distinct from its owners. That means it can hold title to property, sue and be sued, have bank accounts, borrow money, hire employees, and do anything else in the business world that an individual person can do. This entity makes up about eighteen percent of all U.S. businesses but generates about eighty-two percent of the revenues according

VIRGINIA MARC

to the 2012 Statistical Abstract: The National Data Book. Many of these are high-income professionals such as doctors, lawyers, accountants, architects, and dentists, who have formed professional corporations. There are two types of corporations, for which federal income tax rules greatly differ:

- C corporations, sometimes called regular corporations (must pay income taxes on their net income and file their own tax returns with the IRS).
- S corporations, also called small business corporations (is taxed like a sole proprietorship or partnership and is not a separate taxpaying entity).

*Note: S corporations are the most popular types of corporations for a one-person business, primarily because they can result in reduced Social Security and Medicare taxes. C corporations can be better for successful businesses with substantial profits. Lastly you can start out as an S corporation and switch to a C corporation later, or vice versa.

Creating and operating a corporation can be very costly, time consuming, and a bit more troublesome than a sole proprietorship. Now you

STEPS TO LAUNCHING YOUR OWN BUSINESS: A BEGINNER'S GUIDE

are wondering, "how do I know if a corporation is best for me?" Consider these six factors to determine if the corporate form will be a viable choice for you:

1. You want to attract investors or eventually you plan to sell your business.
2. You want to obtain the most "limited liability" you can.
3. You want to reduce clients concerns about hiring you due to fears that they could get in trouble with the IRS or other agencies.
4. You want to save on taxes by taking advantage of tax-free employee fringe benefits.
5. You want to reduce your chances of being audited by the IRS.
6. You want to reduce your Social Security and Medicare taxes.

A principal element of a corporation is limited liability, which means that shareholders may take part in the profits through dividends and stock appreciation but are not personally liable for the company's debts. For this

VIRGINIA MARC

reason, this legal form offers the most protection for an owner's personal assets. Because the IRS typically views a corporation as a separate entity for tax purposes, it is possible to be taxed twice: once when the C-Corp makes a profit, and again when dividends are paid to shareholders. Please take into consideration business related lawsuits such as personal liability for negligence. The people who own a corporation are personally liable for any damages caused by their own "negligence" in conducting a corporation. If you form a corporation that lacks the money or insurance to pay for a legal claim brought against it, the attorney of the person suing you may seek a way to sue you personally, to collect against your personal assets. Also, keep in mind regardless of the legal form you choose, it is recommended to get insurance. An insurer will defend you against business-related lawsuits and pay any settlements or damage awards up to a certain amount, as defined by the insurance policy you choose. However, insurance does not protect you from liability for business debts as you would still be required to repay a loan or a default on a lease.

STEPS TO LAUNCHING YOUR OWN BUSINESS: A BEGINNER'S GUIDE

In case you need an idea of corporations here are examples of well-known C corporations: Microsoft, Coca-Cola, and Apple. Some corporations do business under their names as well as under business names, such as Alphabet Inc., which does business as Google. The major take home is that S corporations combine the benefits of partnerships with the limited liability offered by corporations. C corporations, on the other hand, allow for more flexibility in the number and type of shareholders, as well as different classes of stock. Understanding the differences, advantages, and disadvantages are crucial when deciding to incorporate a business.

Partnerships

If you are not the sole owner of your business, you cannot organize as a sole proprietorship, instead you automatically become a partner in a partnership unless you incorporate or form a limited liability company (LLC). According to Census data eight percent of all businesses in the U.S. are partnerships. Let me back track a little, in some states, including California,

Nevada, New York, and Oregon, certain types of professionals are not allowed to form LLCs. In all states, professionals may setup a special type of partnership called a "registered limited liability partnership" (RLLP). Please be sure to check your state's guidelines regarding legal business forms as these may vary from state to state. The purpose of this guide is to point you in the right direction. Therefore, I will not spend too much time talking about RLLPs and LLCs. The end of this chapter includes a list of resources where you can go to register your business as well as learn more about the distinct types of legal forms. Let us get back on track. A partnership is much the same as a sole proprietorship except that there are two or more owners. However, partners must file IRS Schedule E with their returns, showing their partnership income and deductions. A partnership does have the option of being taxed as a regular C corporation or S corporation by filing IRS Form 2553, Election by a Small Business Corporation. A partnership does not pay payroll taxes on the partners' income or withhold income tax. Partners must pay income taxes and self-employment taxes on their partnership income.

STEPS TO LAUNCHING YOUR OWN BUSINESS: A BEGINNER'S GUIDE

When deciding on a partnership you should consider:

- How each partner will share in the partnership profits or losses.
- How partnership decisions will be made.
- What the duties of each partner will be.
- What if a partner leaves or passes on?
- How disputes will be resolved.

*Note: Although not required by law, it is recommended that you create a written partnership agreement answering these and other questions.

Limited liability corporation (LLC)

First began in the mid-1900s. Every state allows one-person LLCs. When you form an LLC, you classify as a business owner, not an employee. However, if you receive a guaranteed salary or pay from the LLC (instead of a share of the LLC's profits), you will be considered an employee of the LLC and will be subject to income tax withholding and employment taxes. In certain states, individuals involved in certain professions are not allowed

VIRGINIA MARC

to form regular LLCs, instead they must form "professional" LLCs and comply with special rules. This business structure allows the business owner to protect personal assets from the business' liabilities.

IRS rules permit LLC owners to decide for themselves how they want their LLC to taxed. Profits and losses of an LLC are typically taxed as personal income or loss to the members. If the LLC has only one member, the IRS treats it as a sole proprietorship for tax purposes. Profits, losses, and deductions are to be reported on a Schedule C. If the LLC has two or more members, each year it must prepare and file the same tax form used by a partnership – IRS Form 1065, U.S. Return of Partnership Income – showing the allocation of profits, losses, credits, and deductions passed through to the members. The LLC must also prepare and distribute to each member a Schedule K-1 form showing the member's allocations. Owners of LLCs have the option of being taxed as a C or an S corporation by making an "election" to receive corporation tax treatment with the IRS. LLC owners enjoy the same limited liability from business debts and lawsuits as corporation owners. One advantage of LLCs is that they allow more

STEPS TO LAUNCHING YOUR OWN BUSINESS: A BEGINNER'S GUIDE

flexibility to allocate profits and losses among the business's owners than corporations do. To form an LLC, you must file articles of organization with the appropriate state agency, usually the secretary of state.

Okay did I lose you? Do not worry I know it is quite a bit to take in especially if you are doing it alone. So, to make it easy for you, on the next pages I have included charts summarizing these legal forms, their advantages, and disadvantages, to help you analyze which structure best fits your own personal goals. Please use them as a quick guide as you are making your decision. Once you choose the business form that works best for you, then you need to choose a location if you have not already done so. Please do not get discouraged here. Your business does not necessarily have to have a brick-and-mortar location. You can choose to operate solely online. The key thing to understand is that as far as registering your business goes, it means the address you use when filing taxes, receiving important documents from government agencies, or your business bank account.

VIRGINIA MARC

Many small-business owners and entrepreneurs opt to work from home. The advantage to this is that it could save you big money on your taxes by taking the home office deduction, if you meet the IRS' requirements and keep good records. If you use part of your home regularly and exclusively for business-related activity, the IRS lets you write off associated rent, utilities, real estate taxes, repairs, maintenance, and other related expenses. Again, it is highly recommended to check with your state laws when choosing a location.

STEPS TO LAUNCHING YOUR OWN BUSINESS: A BEGINNER'S GUIDE

Table 1

Ways to Organize Your Business		
Type of Entity	**Main Advantages**	**Main Drawbacks**
Sole Proprietor	Simple and inexpensive to create and operate Owner reports profit or loss on his or her personal tax return	Owner personally liable for business debts
General Partnership	Simple and inexpensive to create and operate Owners (partners) report their share of profit or loss on their personal tax returns	Owners (partners) personally liable for business debts

VIRGINIA MARC

Ways to Organize Your Business

Limited Partnership	Limited partners have limited personal liability for business debts if they do not participate in management General partners can raise cash without involving outside investors in management of business	General partners personally liable for business debts More expensive to create than general partnership Suitable for companies that invest in real estate
C Corporation	Owners have limited personal liability for business debts Fringe benefits can be deducted as business expense Corporate profit can be split among owners and corporation, resulting in lower overall tax rate	More expensive to create than partnership or sole proprietorship Paperwork can seem burdensome to some owners Separate taxable entity

STEPS TO LAUNCHING YOUR OWN BUSINESS: A BEGINNER'S GUIDE

Ways to Organize Your Business		
S Corporation	Owners have limited personal liability for business debts Owners report their share of corporate profit or loss on their personal tax returns Owners can use corporate loss to offset income from other sources	More expensive to create than partnership or sole proprietorship More paperwork than for a limited liability company, which offers similar advantages Income must be allocated to owners according to their ownership interests Fringe benefits limited for owners who own more than 2% of shares
Professional Corporation	Owners have no personal liability for malpractice of other owners	More expensive to create than partnership or sole proprietorship Paperwork can seem burdensome to some owners All owners must belong to the same profession

VIRGINIA MARC

Ways to Organize Your Business

Nonprofit Corporation	Corporation may not have to pay income taxes Contributions to certain charitable corporations are tax deductible Fringe benefits can be deducted as business expense	Full tax advantages available only to groups organized for the following purposes: charitable, scientific, educational, literary, religious, testing for public safety, fostering national or international sports competition, and preventing cruelty to children or animals Property transferred to corporation stays there; if corporation ends, property must go to another nonprofit
Limited Liability Company	Owners have limited personal liability for business debts even if they participate in management Profit and loss can be allocated differently than ownership interests IRS rules allow LLCs to choose between being taxed as	More expensive to create than partnership or sole proprietorship A member's entire share of LLC profits may be subject to self-employment tax

STEPS TO LAUNCHING YOUR OWN BUSINESS: A BEGINNER'S GUIDE

Ways to Organize Your Business

	partnership or corporation	
Professional Limited Liability Company	Same advantages as a regular limited liability company Owners have no personal liability for malpractice of other owners Gives state-licensed professionals a way to enjoy those advantages	Same as for a regular limited liability company Members generally must all belong to the same profession or related professions.
Limited Liability Partnership	Mostly of interest to partners in old-line professions, such as law, medicine, and accounting Owners (partners) are not	Unlike a limited liability company or a professional limited liability company, owners (partners) remain personally liable for many types of obligations owed to business creditors, lenders, and landlords Not available in all states

VIRGINIA MARC

Ways to Organize Your Business		
	personally liable for the malpractice of other partners	Often limited to a short list of professions
	Owners report their share of profit or loss on their personal tax returns	

Source: Steingold, Fred S. "Legal Guide for Starting & Running a Small Business." 8th edition, Berkley, CA: Nolo, 2005, pp.29.
Table 2

STEPS TO LAUNCHING YOUR OWN BUSINESS: A BEGINNER'S GUIDE

Choosing a Form of Business

There is no one best business form—and choosing the one that will work best for you can be difficult. It all depends on your goals and preferences. The following chart may help you analyze which business form best furthers your own personal goals.

Goal	Sole Proprietorship	Partnership	LLC	S Corporation	C Corporation
Easiest and cheapest to form and operate	✓	✓			
Simplest tax returns	✓	✓			
Avoid state and federal unemployment taxes	✓	✓	✓		
Deduct losses from your personal taxes	✓	✓	✓	✓	
Distribute high profits	✓	✓	✓	✓	
Limit your personal liability			✓	✓	✓
Added credibility for your business				✓	✓
Save on Social Security taxes				✓	
Retain earnings in business (split income)					✓
Provide tax-deductible benefits to employees, including yourself					✓
Benefit from lower corporate tax rates					✓

Source: Fishman, Stephen. "Working for Yourself Law & Taxes for Independent Contractors, Freelancers & Consultants." 8th edition, Berkley, CA: Nolo, 2011, pp.34.

VIRGINIA MARC

RESOURCE GUIDE:

Websites:

https://www.sba.gov/

https://www.legalzoom.com/

https://www.mycorporation.com/

https://www.nolo.com/

https://www.nolo.com/legal-encyclopedia/form-llc-how-to-organize-llc-30287.html

https://www.rocketlawyer.com/

https://www.bizfilings.com/

Books:

"LLC or Corporation?" 9th Edition By: Anthony Mancuso 2020

"Working for Yourself" 11th Edition By: Stephen Fishman 2018

STEPS TO LAUNCHING YOUR OWN BUSINESS: A BEGINNER'S GUIDE

CHAPTER 3: REGISTER YOUR BUSINESS' NAME

Let us do a quick recap. You have made the conscious decision to start a business. You have your "niche" a specialized segment of the market for a particular kind of product or service. Lastly, you have chosen your business structure (sole proprietorship, partnership, corporation, LLC) and location where you plan on setting up shop. Now it is time to get that business name registered.

Registering a business name is often part of the process of registering separate entities like LLCs and corporations (Inc). If you are operating your business as a sole proprietorship, you are likely going to register your business as an LLC. The question I had when I was journeying on this venture was, "do I need an LLC? The answer is no, but it would be a wise decision to obtain one. What is LLC? LLC stands for "Limited Liability Company," and allows you to operate your business as a separate entity from you personally. In other words, your personal assets are kept

VIRGINIA MARC

separate from your business assets and protect them from your business' debts and liabilities. Under your LLC you can enter contracts, hire employees, open bank accounts, and obtain business licenses and permits. I also had the question of, "do I need to register an INC.?" Just like an LLC, a corporation keeps your personal assets separate from your business assets, providing personal liability protection and shielding your personal assets from your business liabilities. Under both you can open bank accounts, hire employees, etc. What is the difference between and LLC and a corporation (INC)? The key difference between the two is management structure, corporate formalities, and tax flexibility. Corporations must have a board of directors, officers, and shareholders. Corporations also have more formal maintenance requirements than LLCs, requiring annual meeting with corporate minutes. Also, corporations may be subject to double taxation at the business and personal level. In a nutshell, if you are just starting out and operating a small business that does not have substantial profits and are looking for tax flexibility (LLC can choose to be taxed as a sole proprietorship, partnership, S corporation or C corporation depending on the

STEPS TO LAUNCHING YOUR OWN BUSINESS: A BEGINNER'S GUIDE

number of members) you may want to consider an LLC. Corporations can be better for successful businesses with substantial profits. You can always change business entities down the road.

Another question that might come up is, "what if you're starting a sole proprietorship or a partnership operating under a name that isn't your own?" For example, your name is Sarah James, but you want your business name to be something else, you may need to file a DBA (a "doing business as" name). A few states may not require a DBA as part of your business registration. Just make sure before registering your name it is eligible for use. At the end of this chapter, you will find some resources where you can check this. Also, you may want to trademark the name you choose because a DBA does not automatically protect the name from being reused elsewhere. What the what? Trademarking! What is a trademark? A trademark is a word, phrase, symbol, and/or design that identifies and distinguishes the source of the goods of one party from those of others. In

VIRGINIA MARC

simple language a trademark is your unique identifier and set's your product or service apart from those of others. You would want to register a trademark to not only protect the name from being reused elsewhere, but to also secure federal protection from intellectual property assets. The amazing thing about trademarks is that they do not expire so long as you continue to use the mark in commerce to indicate the source of goods and services. How do I know if a trademark is right for me? Say for example, you are creating a swimwear line and you decide you want to call it Soaked (name is made up for demonstration purposes). Soaked is now the brand name of your swimwear line. You have created a beautiful logo and website with the domain name soaked.com. It would be a wise decision to trademark this business name to prevent it from being used anywhere else simply because you have invested time and money in your logo and website. Since we brought up trademarking let me touch on what a patent is. A patent is a limited duration property right relating to an invention, granted by the United States Patent and Trademark Office in exchange for public disclosure of the invention. So maybe your business involves a brand-new

STEPS TO LAUNCHING YOUR OWN BUSINESS: A BEGINNER'S GUIDE

machine, industrial process, chemical composition, or manufactured article you want to get a patent. And then there is copyright. Maybe you plan on publishing a few novels, poetry, movies, music, or computer software, you want to get a copyright to protect your original works of authorship. If you would like to learn more about trademarks, patents, and copyrights please check out https://www.uspto.gov.

The bottom line is registering your business name protects you against infringement, which is defined as the action of breaking the terms of a law, agreement, etc. In other words, it is a major violation. Trademark your business or product name with all the information you need to choose a distinctive mark and register it with USPTO. Before registering a business name or a trademark it is highly recommended that you do a search to make sure the name is not already in use. One way you can do this is by doing a search online using Google or Bing. This option to search is also available on the USPTO website and that is where you would go to trademark your business name. If you need help with setting up an LLC, LegalZoom is a great resource. They walk you through the process step-by-step.

But wait! How much does this all cost? When starting a business, it is important to understand that there will likely be some form of investment involved. There are costs associated with applying for and filing either an LLC or INC. This amount is going to vary from situation to situation and state to state. This amount can range anywhere from forty-nine dollars to hundreds of dollars. At the time of the writing, according to bizfilings.com, the Florida fee for filing an INC is seventy dollars and to file an LLC it is one hundred twenty-five dollars. Just be sure to research your state fees.

Once you have completed this process you need to register your business with the IRS to receive your Employer Identification Number (EIN). Your EIN is like a Social Security number for your business and is necessary for filing your taxes. You can apply for an EIN on the IRS website. Keep in mind, there are certain circumstances where you may not need one and the IRS has a short survey on their website you can fill out to determine if you do. Once all the federal registrations are complete, you

STEPS TO LAUNCHING YOUR OWN BUSINESS: A BEGINNER'S GUIDE

likely need to register your business with one or more agencies in your state or local government, such as revenue offices. If you plan to run payroll, you may also need to register with your state agency to file payroll taxes. Last, make sure you have all the right licenses and permits you need to begin serving customers. Depending on the industry you choose there may be different requirements. Also, you would want to obtain insurance for your business and yourself.

I must admit when I decided I wanted to be an Entrepreneur I found this portion to be the most tedious because there are so many rules and regulations that must be followed. Registering your business is a process and depending on the industry and stipulations can be time consuming. Just remember you do not have to go it alone. If you want this process to go smoothly you can hire help. As previously mentioned, at the end of this chapter you will find some helpful resources to ensure you have a smooth process. You can also seek help from a mentor who has already went

VIRGINIA MARC

through this process to guide you. Feel free to start and stop this guide where necessary as you complete each step in the process.

STEPS TO LAUNCHING YOUR OWN BUSINESS: A BEGINNER'S GUIDE

RESOURCE GUIDE:

Websites:

www.uspto.gov

www.IRS.gov

www.legalzoom.com

www.nolo.com

https://www.sba.gov/business-guide/launch-your-business/get-business-insurance

VIRGINIA MARC

CHAPTER 4: CREATING A BUSINESS PLAN

Give yourself a round of applause. You are making progress. Running a business is not easy but having all the right tools and resources you will have your business up and running whether you are selling in person, online, or both before you know it. Once you have your business name registered you want to make sure you have a business plan in place. Technically this could and should be the first step in the process. However, the idea is to get you to act as opposed to just sitting on an idea. Also, even if you have just an idea and a business name it is important to protect it by getting it registered because once you do that no one else can use it. It would be a slap in the face if you take all that time coming up with a brilliant idea for a business and then by the time you think you got it together you go to register your business only to discover it was already snatched from under you because you did not act fast enough. You can keep a business journal and jot down ideas along the way.

At this point you should be feeling accomplished because you have already taken the necessary steps to get you moving in the right direction.

STEPS TO LAUNCHING YOUR OWN BUSINESS: A BEGINNER'S GUIDE

Now that you have your business name registered, are you ready to open for business? With owning a business comes great responsibility and budgeting. So, I am sharing with you some things you should take into consideration.

1. How will my business help others? Remember you are not in business for yourself you are in business to provide solutions this is what will keep you in business for the long haul.
2. How will my business generate income?
3. How much will I need to invest weekly/monthly to make sure my business thrives?
4. How much time should I invest in my business?
5. What would be my daily goal to make a healthy profit? (Number of sales per day needed to reach goal and meet budget)
6. How much will I spend in over-head charges monthly?
   - Lease (if leasing an office space)

VIRGINIA MARC

- Utilities (Electric, Water, Cable, Phone, Internet)
- Marketing (Website, business cards, flyers, email marketing)
- Office supplies
- Free or purchased leads

7. Do you plan on hiring a team to help run your business? If this will be the case, you may want to assess your network for the following roles and commit to expand where needed:
    a) Team – People who help bring my dreams to life.
    b) Support – People who care for my well-being.
    c) Sponsors – People who connect me to opportunities.
    d) Advisers – Accomplished people with sound insight.
    e) Proteges – People who can learn from me.
    f) Rabbits – People who show what is possible for my next business endeavor.
8. Do I plan on using social media (YouTube, Facebook, Instagram, LinkedIn, Pinterest, etc.)?
9. Who will be my target audience?

STEPS TO LAUNCHING YOUR OWN BUSINESS: A BEGINNER'S GUIDE

10. Setting up a rudimentary bookkeeping system. According to Investopedia the following are the five best accounting software for small businesses of twenty-twenty.

    - QuickBooks Online: Best Overall
    - Xero: Best for Micro-Business Owners
    - FreshBooks: Best for Service-Based Businesses
    - QuickBooks Self-Employed: Best for Part-time Freelancers
    - Wave: Best Free Software

The overall goal here is to have a plan set in place and you want to make sure to execute it effectively.

VIRGINIA MARC

CHAPTER 5: SOCIAL MEDIA

Are you ready to launch your business? Let us check our list:

1. Choose a product or service to sell (find your niche)
2. Choose the legal form or entity for your business
3. Choose a business name, register your name, and get a trademark or patent if necessary
4. Register your business with the IRS to get an Employer Identification Number (EIN) for tax filing purposes
5. Register with state and local agencies, especially if you plan to run payroll
6. Obtain a business license and permit
7. Obtain insurance for your business and for yourself
8. Setup a rudimentary bookkeeping system

If you have completed these steps, you are making excellent progress. If you are half-way there, keep up the good work. The key is getting started. Remember the little steps you take lead to bigger progress.

STEPS TO LAUNCHING YOUR OWN BUSINESS: A BEGINNER'S GUIDE

With a proper plan of action, you will be surprised at what you can accomplish.

Let us get down to business. In this chapter we will discuss social media and how your business can benefit from it. With the increase in use of technology, today so many business owners are utilizing the social media platforms to put their business in front of a larger audience. You cannot deny the fact that so many people are constantly on their smartphones. In fact, for many of us smartphones have replaced traditional landline phones. According to a website known as broad band search, in the year of twenty-twenty roughly three point eight million people use social media and on average we spend two hours and twenty-four minutes on social media. The fact of the matter is social media can be a powerful tool to help leverage your business. But just as helpful as social media can be for business, it can also hurt your business. Just be mindful you are operating a business therefore you want to always maintain professional.

VIRGINIA MARC

On social media your image is everything. Look at it this way you just transitioned into a fearless boss and business owner, so it is important to look like the boss you truly are. Therefore, you need to position yourself as a boss on social media. Social media can basically act as your lead magnet. If you already are not utilizing social media, you might be wondering which platform is best for you. Allow me to take a moment to highlight the top seven social media sites:

1. **Instagram**

   - Primarily utilized by small business owners, brands, bloggers, and influencers.
   - Well over one billion users.
   - Great if your customers are under the age of forty.
   - Suggested content: eye-capturing photography, beautiful visuals, unique designs, selfie-style video that speaks directly to your audience.

   Growth Strategies

   - Posting Daily – Multiple Times

STEPS TO LAUNCHING YOUR OWN BUSINESS: A BEGINNER'S GUIDE

- Using Hashtags
- Commenting
- Use Video Content
- Post in the Stories
- Shout Outs & Shares
- Running Ads for Content vs. Sales

2. **YouTube**

- Reaches close to two billion users (sixty-eight countries and over seventy languages)
- Americans spend an average of forty minutes per day on YouTube
- Reaches ninety-five percent of all adults aged thirty-five plus online
- Gen X, Baby Boomers, & Millennials
- Fifty-six percent of those fifty-five plus use YouTube

VIRGINIA MARC

- Millennials prefer YouTube 2x More Than Traditional TV
- Thirty-seven percent of those age eighteen to thirty-four use YouTube to Binge Watch Content
- Seventy percent watch on mobile
- Easy & Inexpensive to Run Ads
- Great to use if your business could benefit from producing video tutorials and how to DIYs (Do It Yourself), visually driven instructional content, product reviews or interviews
- Video-only content works best on this platform

Growth Strategies

- Promoting on Platforms Outside of YouTube
- Consistent Content
- Production Formula → Sample – three-to-seven-minute attention grabber, bumper, content, engagement, exit, and CTA
- Optimize Video after You Upload
- Keywords
- Collaboration Opportunities

STEPS TO LAUNCHING YOUR OWN BUSINESS: A BEGINNER'S GUIDE

- Brokerage firms
- YouTube Values Watch Time over Metadata

3. **Facebook**

- Nearly two point five billion users (U.S. adults make up sixty-eight percent with fifty-one percent active users)
- Great if your customers are primarily above the age of thirty
- Leverage Facebook groups to gather customers or community in one place online
- Leverage Facebook business pages for advertising
- Great to use if you want to reach an audience of adults and have engaging visual (or video) content that can capture their attention, invoke an immediate emotional response, and make them excited to share with their friends

Growth Strategies

- Posting Daily

VIRGINIA MARC

- Engaging with others
- Ask Questions
- Use Video Content
- Ads Do Help
- Working Groups

4. **Twitter**

- Estimated three hundred million users (sixty-three percent are between ages of thirty-five and sixty-five with males making up about two-thirds of those people)
- Ideal for bite-sized content and direct communication with your users in real-time (videos and images stand out best)

Growth Strategies

- Tweet frequently.
- Optimize your posting time.
- Post visual content.
- Utilize hashtags.
- Engage with replies, re-tweets, and tags.

STEPS TO LAUNCHING YOUR OWN BUSINESS: A BEGINNER'S GUIDE

- Create an inviting profile.
- Identify followers within your network.
- Draw in followers outside of Twitter.

5. **TikTok**

- There is an estimate of eight hundred million users (fifty percent under the age of thirty-five in U.S. majority range in age sixteen to twenty-four)
- Ideal content should be entertaining, comedic, interesting, and short-form video. You want to think fun, catchy music-video style content.
- Utilize this content if you want to reach a young audience.

Growth Strategies

- Engage with content that compliments your brand. Follow influencers that would be great partners for your brand and engage in their videos.

- Use TikTok Ads. With these Ads you can target a specific demographics and locations to make sure your content reaches the most relevant audiences, which could mean plenty of conversions into new followers.
- Repost TikTok as user-generated content. This can also help with boosting your posting frequency.
- Collaborate with content creators.
- Connect to your other social media channels to cross-promote.

6. **Pinterest**
- Immensely popular social bookmarking tool for saving ideas and finding creative inspiration from cooking to DIY home projects, vacation ideas, interior design, business, and everything in between.
- Roughly over three hundred twenty million users (eighty percent female).
- The content that works best here are polished imagery with clear copy that conveys what the pinner will see if they click through.

STEPS TO LAUNCHING YOUR OWN BUSINESS: A BEGINNER'S GUIDE

Numbers, lists, and quotes should be a big part of your strategy here.

- Utilize this platform if your audience is predominantly women and your business is related to lifestyle, fashion, decorating, or DIY.

Growth Strategies

- Be active and engage on Pinterest
    - Manually pinning on a regular basis
    - Go to the "Explore" and "Trending" pages and re-pin from there
    - Pin other people's pins manually
    - When you see a "Board to Follow" in your feed, follow them if they are relevant.
- Follow your competitor's follower
- Utilize the search bar

VIRGINIA MARC

- Use hashtags
- Start your own group board
- Craft compelling infographics

7. **Linked-In**

- Five hundred million users
- Two hundred fifty million monthly active users
- One hundred thirty-three million U.S. users
- Forty percent of Linked-in Users use it daily
- Fifty-seven percent male & forty-three percent female users
- Thirteen percent of Millennials use Linked-In
- Forty-four percent of Linked-in users earn seventy-five thousand dollars or more per year
- About forty million students and recent grads on Linked-In
- Forty-one percent of Millionaires use LinkedIn
- One million professionals have published post on their Linked-In
- What are they doing? → Seeking Jobs, Recruiting, Business Development, Sales, Businessmen and Businesswomen

STEPS TO LAUNCHING YOUR OWN BUSINESS: A BEGINNER'S GUIDE

Growth Strategies

- Posting Daily

- Creating Articles, Blogs, and Vlogs

- Networking in groups

- Using the DM (Direct Messenger)

- Endorsements

By now you should be able to narrow down which platform will work best for you. The takeaway from this is how you present yourself on these platforms will play a major role in who you attract. You are creating an image for yourself while building a brand. Most people are not really trying to buy what it is you are selling especially when they can get it from somewhere else. Therefore, the idea is to build a relationship with your audience and connect with them to make them want to sew into your business. Instead of trying to convince people to purchase your product or service, they should naturally be attracted to whatever it is you have to offer.

VIRGINIA MARC

Image speaks volumes and you only get once chance to make a lasting impression. My advice to you would be do not prematurely launch your business on social media if you have not figured it all out yet. What is meant by that? Before you introduce your business to the world on social media you want to make sure you have completed the necessary steps mentioned above for starters. Also, you want to make sure your product or service is ready to launch. Since people are so drawn to visuals when it comes to social media, a nice catchy business logo could carry you far and you want to make sure your theme and the content you create leaves a good lasting impression. Here are some things you can do to make a good lasting impression on social media. One rule that you must follow is to be professional at all times. Position yourself like the boss you are. If you look like you are successful people are going to want to know more about what it is, you have to offer. Position yourself as a leader. Another rule of thumb is to separate your personal life from your business life. Do not get me wrong, it is okay to share a little bit of your personal life this is how you build a connection with your audience but sharing too much of the wrong

STEPS TO LAUNCHING YOUR OWN BUSINESS: A BEGINNER'S GUIDE

information can be bad for business. Also, it would be entirely up to you if you choose to setup a separate account for personal and business.

On the flip side, if social media seems to be too complicated you may want to consider hiring someone to manage your social media accounts. Just before I bring this topic to a close, allow me to mention that if you do plan on using social media and already have a name for your business you may want to lock in those names before they are already taken. The great thing about these platforms is that you can create multiple pages. Now we are ready to talk about how to put your business on automation, especially if you are a one-man band.

VIRGINIA MARC

CHAPTER 6: AUTOMATE YOUR BUSINESS

Probably one of the most difficult tasks with starting a business, is running it. Are you a one-man show or do you have a team to help with the heavy lifting? This step is more for those who are the only operators of their business. However, even if you have a staff, you may still find this to be beneficial.

There are many individuals who start up a business but are still working a nine to five. Trying to make time for both can be a tedious task especially if you are single parent trying to raise a family. If you are working a nine to five that means you have from five to nine to work your business. Anyone could easily get burnt out especially if you are in a line of business that calls for serious attention. Take into consideration marketing, sending emails, responding to emails, following up with clients, inventory if you are dealing with a product, collecting payments, creating invoices, and appointments if you offer a service. This is where setting up a system allows you to take a little bit of the load off. To my social media users, have you ever been strolling down your timeline and then suddenly notice an ad that is

STEPS TO LAUNCHING YOUR OWN BUSINESS: A BEGINNER'S GUIDE

promoting some sort of product or service? If you were as curious as me, you clicked on the ad, usually a button that says, "learn more", and it brought you to a page that prompted you to enter your information. What you experienced is something that many businesses are using to help capture leads. This is how they get interested prospects to turn into paying customers. That form you saw is something known as a funnel. Once the client enters their information, they are usually redirected to a thank you page or a page offering a sale which requires the consumer to put in his/her payment information, or to join a webinar of some sort. Many businesses are successful with running a one-page funnel. These funnels are less complicated than a website in that it leads your prospect directly to what it is you have to offer, instead of them fishing around. With these funnels some businesses are even generating sales in their sleep. Another great thing about these funnels is that they are typically low cost to run and operate and requires little to no maintenance. This is convenient to help you run your business if you do not have additional funds to hire employees. Most of these systems have autoresponder emails built in that will automatically send out emails to your clients when they visit your capture page, issue an invoice whenever a purchase is made, or even send a request. One of my personal favorites I have used is HBA Funnel Builder. HBA stands for Home Business Academy. On the home page you will find an informative introduction video. Once you sign up and begin using their service, you will find step-by-step video tutorials to help get your system setup. There are so many templates to choose from which makes it easy for you to create a functional lead generating funnel. At the time of me writing this the cost for the service is twenty-five dollars per month but they do offer a referral program that earns you a twenty-dollar residual commission for as long as whoever uses your link to sign up stays enrolled. When you think about it twenty-five dollars is a small price to pay when you earn a life-time commission that will enable you to cover the monthly charge. It is like getting a free service to help drive traffic to your business whereas most companies charge hundreds or even thousands of dollars for similar systems.

STEPS TO LAUNCHING YOUR OWN BUSINESS: A BEGINNER'S GUIDE

This one was my personal choice because I found it super easy to use so much so that even the technically challenged individual would not find it too difficult. This system does not have an email autoresponder system, but it does allow you to sync one of your choosing. Why do you need an autoresponder email service? This system allows you to create a sequence of emails sent automatically to people in your email list. For example, if you are collecting email addresses on a "coming soon page", then you can set up an autoresponder to send a sequence of emails when your website goes live. Perhaps you are a blogger, and you want to welcome new subscribers, an autoresponder sequence will do all the work for you. Let us look at some of the most popular autoresponder tools that can be of assistance to you:

1. ActiveCampaign
    - Free trial available
    - Includes automation

VIRGINIA MARC

- Integration with services (Shopify, BigCommerce, WooCommerce, etc.)
- Offers reporting on areas such as click-maps, geo-tracking, and page visits.
- Costs is nine dollars per month for the "Lite" plan upward to two hundred twenty-five dollars for "Enterprise" plan.

2. Constant Contact
   - Sixty-day free trial (there is no free forever plan available and to use most of the automated features after trial you will need to pay for the plus plan)
   - Does not require credit card details only billed if choose to use service.
   - Can set up your email design based on website branding by scanning your site to find images and colors.
   - Hundreds of templates to choose from.
   - Easy to set up account.

STEPS TO LAUNCHING YOUR OWN BUSINESS: A BEGINNER'S GUIDE

- Plan costs twenty dollars per month for basic and forty-five dollars for plus plan with advanced features.

3. Sendinblue

    - Combines both email and SMS marketing
    - Allows unlimited contacts on the free plan (limited by how many emails you can send out each day).
    - Access to email support on free plan.
    - Drag and drop interface with wide range of templates available or create your own (upload an HTML template if you have already created one separately).
    - Three hundred email limit per day.
    - Costs is free but if you want more features you can upgrade to paid plan twenty-five dollars per month.

4. MailerLite

VIRGINIA MARC

- Plenty of features available on the free plan (landing pages, multi-user accounts, and A/B split testing of emails).
- Free plan does not limit you to a set number of emails per day but there is a monthly limit of twelve thousand emails.
- Cheapest paid plan gives you access to all the "premium plans" features.
- Drag and drop editor to create emails.
- No email templates available on free plan.
- Free plan allows for one thousand contacts
- Logo cannot be removed on free plan.
- Costs is ten dollars per month on lowest plan but for more subscribers you will need to pay fifteen dollars per month or more.

5. AWeber
    - Founded in nineteen ninety-eight (most established autoresponder tool out there)
    - Free thirty-day trial includes all premium features.

STEPS TO LAUNCHING YOUR OWN BUSINESS: A BEGINNER'S GUIDE

- Powerful automation and segmentation tools.
- Can be integrated with huge number of other services (PayPal, Unbounce, OptinMonster, etc.)
- Master class sessions and live webinars available.
- New features are added regularly available to all users.
- Costs is nineteen dollars per month (five hundred subscribers), twenty-nine dollars per month (more than five hundred subscribers), or forty-nine dollars per month (twenty-five hundred or more)

6. Mailchimp

    - Free plan offers segmentation and simple autoresponders (email support available only for first thirty days).
    - Integrates with over three hundred apps (Canva, Help Scout, HBA funnel builder, etc.)
    - Drag and drop templates easy to set up and modify.

- Built in CRM tool.
- Cannot create multi-step autoresponder sequences on the "Free" or "Essentials" plans.
- Costs is nine ninety-nine per month for the "Essentials" plan or "pay as you go" from one hundred fifty dollars for five thousand emails.

7. ConvertKit
    - Free plan allows unlimited landing pages and opt-in forms. Also offers a fourteen-day free trial to use premium features such as automation functionality.
    - Allows you to segment customers and assign tags.
    - Landing page builder with thirty templates to choose from.
    - When you invite friends to use this service you unlock most of the features of the free plan.
    - Costs is twenty-nine dollars per month (one thousand subscribers) or forty-nine dollars per month (up to three thousand subscribers).

STEPS TO LAUNCHING YOUR OWN BUSINESS: A BEGINNER'S GUIDE

8. Get Response

- Does not have a free plan but offers thirty-day free trial.

- Can be integrated with many services (ClickBank, PayPal, OptinMonster, Shopify, etc.)

- Support is available via phone, live chat, and email.

- Most affordable plan costs fifteen dollars per month (up to one thousand subscribers).

So now you might be wondering which autoresponder tool would be best for you. Use your better judgement. Do keep in mind when you are building a business, you want to make sure you have access to top notch support and a powerful platform. Also, be mindful of your budget and what you can invest. There are plenty of great funnel building tools out there as well to choose from, so I encourage you to do your research to find what best suits your needs.

VIRGINIA MARC

If funnels are not your thing you can result to traditional websites. Do keep in mind, especially if you are just starting out and are on a very tight budget, these can be very costly, and time consuming to maintain. One thing I do love about websites though is that you can monetize your site with pay-per-click links, ads, and other sorts of affiliate marketing. Just a way to earn extra cash. There are free options to build a site such as Wix, Weebly, and WordPress to name a few. But, in my opinion these are great if you are tech savvy. If going the free route just be sure to get a domain name and register it with the web host for your site because usually the free sites have long domain names. For example, if you run a bakery business and you called your business Sweet Cakes you would want to choose a domain name like sweetcakes.com. Usually, when you use Wix site you will be given a domain name something along the lines of www.wixsite/sweetcakes.com. This is just for demonstration purposes, but you should get the general idea. Regardless of the system and tools you choose to utilize, the goal is to automate your business so that it simplifies

STEPS TO LAUNCHING YOUR OWN BUSINESS: A BEGINNER'S GUIDE

the way you do business enabling you to earn money while you sleep, work, and play.

VIRGINIA MARC

CHAPTER 7: CHOOSING & PRICING YOUR PRODUCT/SERVICE

You have invested time and money in getting your business up and running so you want to make sure your business is giving you a healthy return. Now this step could go in conjunction with finding your niche as well as creating a business plan. However, I felt it was necessary to dedicate an entire chapter to choosing and pricing your product/service.

The focus is on product variation and selection. Often time as creators and consultants we forget that different people learn in different ways and have a desire for different levels of service. Someone who wants something customized for them and is not interested in learning how something works and wants something that can be applied specifically to their situation or to their desires would be a good candidate for a one-on-one elite program, something that allows you to work with them directly. For clients who think they can figure things out themselves and just need a little direction or maybe it does not fit inside of their budget to have a customize level of service are good candidates for mid-range and low-cost products. For your true priors and low-cost products, you will find that this is a great way to

STEPS TO LAUNCHING YOUR OWN BUSINESS: A BEGINNER'S GUIDE

develop your higher end clients because often time they need to be able to get comfortable with you, the company, the processes, the team, etc. Once they see that the products are what you say they are and are getting some sort of result or some type of understanding, they are willing to join you inside of other different products or have you come and provide additional services for them.

It is important that whenever we think about what product or what desire we want to help our client accomplish we figure out more than one way to help them do this. It can be the same "thing", but we need to figure out at least three different ways to do that "thing" because there is going to be three types of clients who are attracted to us. So, the first variation of that product is going to be your super low-cost version of it, aka your true-prior. It is a deal that is difficult to refuse. It is almost so good that people cannot believe that they are getting it at that rate. Also, this is a great way to get new people turned on to your services or products. The second variation

VIRGINIA MARC

of the product is going to be anything that is a mid-range or even a low-cost product. These are going to be affordable; it is a way to help clients get quick fixes, a way to continue to establish yourself as a resource, a great way to build a strong working relationship with the client, and it is a good way to create another transaction for repeat customers because we want frequency. Lastly, the third variation is where you are going to offer your customization. This is when you are working with clients directly, one-on-one. This maybe where you work with the clients directly as opposed to having someone else on your team to work with them. This could be where you come in and personally manage their accounts and take care of their affairs, communicate with them, and provide troubleshooting and resolution services for them. Think about the fact there is only one you. So, anytime you specifically are managing, directing, helping, assisting, building, or strategizing with a client that is going to have a premium price point because you are working to help them achieve their specific desired outcome. If you are doing anything that is in a group setting or maybe one of your company's representatives or a contractor for you is in the mix, that is going

STEPS TO LAUNCHING YOUR OWN BUSINESS: A BEGINNER'S GUIDE

to have a little bit of a lower price point associated with it because they do not have direct access to you, or you may not be specifically speaking with or handling that client's account or affairs every time there is an interaction between them and the company. Then, our Lower tier-products and services are going to be those things such as e-books, workshops, or repetitive services.

Okay, so let us discuss some examples. I am going to use a salon owner. As a salon owner you are maybe providing clients with a facial every two weeks or every quarter as well as making sure you are washing, trimming, and styling their hair. Those are reoccurring things that do not have large price points and you are continuing to show that you are a resource, that you are an expert, and that you are a professional. Whatever it is that you are helping your client or customer with I want you to think about, what is the overall result people would like to achieve. Think about what service you could provide, consultancy, or if there is a digital product

VIRGINIA MARC

if you are a coach or even a physical product if you are a service provider. Let us revisit the example of the salon owner, you could sell the products that you use inside of the salon. Maybe it is a product to help your clients maintain their skin, hair, or body weight. Or maybe if you are a fitness coach or instructor you could come up with meal plans or nutritional guides for your clients. Those are ways to add additional revenue streams for yourself and for your business, it is a great way to help your clients achieve optimal results. It is a win-win for everyone.

So, think about what it is you help your clients do, what their desired results are in diff variations of that specific product. Something else to keep in mind, I call it the full product spectrum. A lot of times when we are meeting people whether in person and especially on the social media stratosphere, people need to warm up to you if you are a service provider, consultant, or a coach. If you are involved in an MLM you have so much competition, there are so many other people trying to get others to join the team or purchase products. Therefore, you really need to do a good job of building and nurturing a relationship this is where your lead magnets come

STEPS TO LAUNCHING YOUR OWN BUSINESS: A BEGINNER'S GUIDE

into play. So, think about the overall goal. Say for example, you are involved in network marketing maybe you have a jewelry company, and you would like people to join your team, you cannot convolute building your team with selling the actual jewelry, you have two separate desires you must focus on. When it comes time to building the team, we can say hey this is a great way you can make additional income and stay fashionable. Let me give you ten ways that you can build your clientele when you decide to work from home. That is going to be your lead magnet so you can start to develop a relationship with those people who would be good candidates to join the team. Maybe after they get your free e-book or download "10 Ways to Build Clientele", at the end you say hey I would love to sign you up for a discovery session and we can talk about some of your financial goals, how much time you are able dedicate to the business and let us try and put together a plan for you so you can be successful. Now you can get them on the phone talk about your company, the great benefits of it and why they

VIRGINIA MARC

should specifically be a member of your team. The end goal is to get them to come and be a part of your family. You could also mention how you are going to provide them with continued education, different sells training, bringing in other experts to help them grow and develop their social media, their client basis, product training all those sorts of things. You must differentiate yourself.

Now on the other side you have the issue of now "I have to sell this physical product. I have jewelry to sell". So maybe your freebie to the customer that you are selling the jewelry to would be eight ways to rock one necklace or 5 ways to dress up any look or to take it from daytime to nighttime just with switching your accessories. Maybe you want to provide a style guide or trend guide for the summer or for the fall depending on what season you are rolling into and of course show case your company's products and give people links on where they can purchase them. Periodically while you are inside of your stories on your Facebook page or Instagram page, you are showing the new jewelry as it comes in. Maybe

STEPS TO LAUNCHING YOUR OWN BUSINESS: A BEGINNER'S GUIDE

you are doing un-boxings during your livestreams to generate sales of the physical products.

So, we must think about something that we can give to a client for free. In MLM again your focus is on growing your team. How can I get more people to join my team, how can I help people make more money, how can I help them create their client base and grow their team, how can I create a support system for them so that I can take the fear and anxiety away from them of doing something new? So, for a service provider, like the salon owner we mentioned earlier, I am going to think about what I am going to do to get a new client in because women are very particular about our hairstylist and who we go to for our skincare and our beauty regimens and those types of things. Let us use natural hair clients as an example, maybe I will give them a guide for natural hair offering something such as 10 protective styles you can do in 30 minutes or less or how to protect your hair underneath your wigs and weaves to obtain optimal growth. Those are great

VIRGINIA MARC

lead magnets to give to your clients so now that you are establishing yourself as a resource and an expert and after they get that maybe you could offer them a low-cost product. Maybe you discussed specific oils or mixtures or you have your own conditioner that you make for your salon and you could say, "hey you could order this or grab this right now" or after they get the lead magnet you could redirect them to a page that says, "hey we're taking new clients and we'll give you twenty percent off your first visit or we'll give you a free eyebrow shape up when you get your hair done". Anything that is going to attract and cultivate those new clients to come in through the door. If you are a coach or consultant, again think about what the overall product is. Maybe you have a new academy you are about to launch, and you really want to try and see if you can get fifteen to twenty people to come into this new academy that you are having so you can make sure that you can get all the kinks out of it to really provide an excellent experience and work in your full capacity. Because maybe you decided that one-on-one is not for you so you really would prefer to work in a small group setting. So, if you are a coach or consultant again you want to

STEPS TO LAUNCHING YOUR OWN BUSINESS: A BEGINNER'S GUIDE

provide a helpful lead magnet. Say for example, you help writers and authors. A good suggestion would be to provide something such as seven things I wish I knew before I started writing my first book or ten things the publishing companies do not want you to know. You would offer that as a free item. Once people get the freebie then you could offer them one of your "pay ninety-nine" products. That purchase product could be "the ultimate guide to self-publishing" or "the ultimate guide to selling more books". After they purchase that product and enjoy it you can invite them into a webinar or live session and give an amazing training and at the end of the training you could invite them to join a program where you are offering a twelve-week one-on-one session on writing, publishing, and selling books. The idea is to think about the full product spectrum.

When you are creating product variations, you must make sure you are thinking about the overall product spectrum. From the freebie to how you convert that person into a lead and then how you present an offer, a higher

VIRGINIA MARC

cost product or service to them. You also need to think about the different levels of customization that clients are going to require because not everyone is going to work with you inside of your academy. Everyone is not going to work with you one-on-one. If you are a fitness trainer, for example and I really love coming to your classes, but on the flip side I could be one who is self-conscious because I just had a baby and I feel uncomfortable working out with everyone else. Maybe I want you to come to my house and help me get myself together in private. Think about what the clients and customers want from you and then think about product or product line or what service or service line you want to focus on for right now. That is not to say you can only sell one thing at a time but what I am saying is that you must focus on making one offer to one set of clients. You cannot try and sell everything to everyone. If I am opening enrollment for one-on-one clients for people who want to work with me directly, that is a completely different pitch then when I say, "hey who wants to come to this workshop?" There are going to be way more people who want to come to the workshop and can afford to come to a free workshop than there are

STEPS TO LAUNCHING YOUR OWN BUSINESS: A BEGINNER'S GUIDE

people who can afford to pay ten thousand dollars or fifteen thousand dollars to consult with me on a one-on-one basis every month throughout the year helping them put together a customized strategy. If you try and sell to everyone you sell to no one. Think about the product or a service. Think about who needs that product or service. From there create your product variations and determine how you are going to make offers to those people. The following pages will provide you with some worksheets to help you brainstorm if you are still struggling with trying to come up with product ideas as well as product pricing.

VIRGINIA MARC

Brainstorm

What is your Industry?

_____

_____

_____

What is your product or program?

_____

_____

_____

What is your hobby or what do you have fun doing?

_____

_____

STEPS TO LAUNCHING YOUR OWN BUSINESS: A BEGINNER'S GUIDE

PRODUCT IDEAS

What products or services are the most popular in your industry?

_____

_____

_____

_____

Top 20 -- Are these products that already exist? Are they ideas?

1. _____
2. _____
3. _____
4. _____
5. _____
6. _____
7. _____
8. _____

VIRGINIA MARC

9._____
10._____
11._____
12._____
13._____
14._____
15._____
16._____
17._____
18._____
19._____
20._____

STEPS TO LAUNCHING YOUR OWN BUSINESS: A BEGINNER'S GUIDE

Archetype Guide: Who Is My Customer?

What's your person's name? (Imagine a potential client in front of you, what is their name?)

_____

What is the age range of your potential clients? (18-23) (28-59)

_____

What is their marital status?

_____

What is their education level?

_____

What are their hobbies & Favorite TV shows? (list 5)

_____

VIRGINIA MARC

_____

_____

_____

What music do they listen to? (Genre, band, artist, etc.)

_____

_____

_____

What do they do for a living?

_____

_____

STEPS TO LAUNCHING YOUR OWN BUSINESS: A BEGINNER'S GUIDE

Product Pricing Guide

How Much Is This?

Pricing Basics – How much is your base price

What is your Overhead? Overhead expenses are all **costs** on the income statement except for direct labor, direct materials, and direct expenses. **Overhead** expenses include accounting fees, advertising, insurance, interest, legal fees, labor burden, rent, repairs, supplies, taxes, telephone bills, travel expenditures, and utilities.

Add up your overhead cost for next month or an average. What is the number_____ How many anticipated clients or sales do you think you will make? _____

Fixed Cost = Monthly overhead / Number of Sales_____

This is the minimum cost your products should be priced at.

VIRGINIA MARC

Now to the Direct Materials cost. Direct material cost is the **cost** of the raw **materials** and components used to create a product. The **materials** must be easily identifiable with the resulting product (otherwise they are joint **costs**)

List all the components needed to create one unity of your product. Add them together and place the number here. _____

Labor Cost. Direct labor cost is a part of wage-bill or payroll that can be specifically and consistently assigned to or associated with the manufacture of a product, a particular work order, or provision of a service.

Are you paying yourself or anyone else hourly rates? What is the rate associated with one unit of your product?

(Hours of work x hourly rate) / units produced = Labor Rate per Unit.

Write your Labor cost per unit here _____

Shipping expense is an **expense** incurred that varies directly with the shipping of the products. What is the shipping cost per unity?

Cost of Shipping/ Units Shipped = Unit Shipping Cost.

Write it Here _____

STEPS TO LAUNCHING YOUR OWN BUSINESS: A BEGINNER'S GUIDE

Base Cost of Product = Fixed Cost + Direct materials Cost + Labor Cost per Unit + Shipping per unit _____

Now Add the Margin or Profit you would like to make from each unit sale.

This is the price of your product.

Base Cost + Desired Profit =_____ **(cost of your product)**

VIRGINIA MARC

Service Pricing Guide

How Much Is This?

Pricing Basics – **How much is your base price**

What is your Overhead? Overhead expenses are all **costs** on the income statement except for direct labor, direct materials, and direct expenses.

Overhead expenses include accounting fees, advertising, insurance, interest, legal fees, labor burden, rent, repairs, supplies, taxes, telephone bills, travel expenditures, and utilities.

Add up your overhead cost for next month or an average. What is the number_____

How many anticipated clients or sales do you think you will make?

_____

Fixed Cost = Monthly overhead / Number of Clients

This is the minimum cost your products should be priced at.

Calculate Your Hourly Rate: desired amount you would like to make monthly or annually is what I like to use. The average work week has 2000

STEPS TO LAUNCHING YOUR OWN BUSINESS: A BEGINNER'S GUIDE

hours in it. As a consultant or coach 50% of that time is spent looking for new clients. To ensure you are paid when you are generating business as well, I would advise you calculate your working hours as 1000 to get your hourly rate **Desired Annual Income/ Annual Working Hours= Hourly Rate**

Example: $50,000 annual salary/1500 working hours

$50000/1500=$33.33 per hour

Estimate how many hours of work the project will take. To get the total hours per project.

Labor Cost. Direct labor cost is a part of wage-bill or payroll that can be specifically and consistently assigned to or associated with the manufacture of a product, a particular work order, or provision of a service.

Are you paying yourself or anyone else hourly rates? What is the rate associated with one unit of your product? **(Hours of work x hourly rate) /**

VIRGINIA MARC

units produced = Labor Rate per Unit. Write your Labor cost per unit

here _____

Service Fee = Fixed Cost + Labor Cost per Unit + Total estimated hours

_____

Now Add the Margin or Profit you would like to make from each unit sale.

This is the price of your product.

Service Fee + Desired Profit = _____ **(cost of your services)**

STEPS TO LAUNCHING YOUR OWN BUSINESS: A BEGINNER'S GUIDE

Digital Product Pricing Guide

How Much Is This?

Pricing Basics – How much is your base price

What is your Overhead? Overhead expenses are all **costs** on the income statement except for direct labor, direct materials, and direct expenses. **Overhead** expenses include accounting fees, advertising, insurance, interest, legal fees, labor burden, rent, repairs, supplies, taxes, telephone bills, travel expenditures, and utilities.

Add up your overhead cost for next month or an average. What is the number_____

How many anticipated clients or sales do you think you will make?

_____

Fixed Cost = Monthly overhead / Number of Clients

This is the minimum cost your products should be priced at.

VIRGINIA MARC

Labor Cost. Direct labor cost is a part of wage-bill or payroll that can be specifically and consistently assigned to or associated with the manufacture of a product, a particular work order, or provision of a service.

Are you paying yourself or anyone else hourly rates? What is the rate associated with one unit of your product? **(Hours of work x hourly rate) / units produced = Labor Rate per Unit. Write your Labor cost per unit here** _____

Cost of Software or Digital Hosting: This is the cost of any CRM, Software, Carts, cost per sale, etc. for selling your digital product. Total these cost _____.

Cost of software/Estimated Sales = Host Cost _____

Desired Profit from digital product / projected or estimated sales _____

Digital Product Cost = Fixed Cost + Labor Cost during development & customer service + Host cost + Desired profit

_____

STEPS TO LAUNCHING YOUR OWN BUSINESS: A BEGINNER'S GUIDE

Special Note. When selling digital products be sure to check competitors and see their pricing. You do not want to price yourself out of the market.

VIRGINIA MARC

Product Variation

What is your core product or service?

_____

_____

How do they prefer to consume information? (Put an x by all that apply) What is the most basic form of the product or service?

_____

_____

How will you try to sell this product or service? (Webinar, live event, booth, show, leads group, membership, audio file, e-book, etc.)

_____

(If you are using a presentation, webinar, demonstration, or samples this is valuable info you can use to create a bundle)

Do you have any existing product or service that adds value to the core product? If so, what is it?

STEPS TO LAUNCHING YOUR OWN BUSINESS: A BEGINNER'S GUIDE

_____

_____

Can you create anything to add value to your product or service? (t-shirt, mug, challenge, membership, live or online workshop, audio files, workbook, etc.)

_____

_____

Is there any level of customization or 1-on-1 you can create to add value to the product or service?

_____

_____

List your base product or service here _____

List what you are offering with your base product or service here (this can be a training, physical product, additional service, audio file, e-book, e-

VIRGINIA MARC

course, guide, live event access, etc.)

_____

List your base product or service with an extra element here (one-on-one, customized element, unique system, additional services, loyalty program, direct access, after hours, etc.)

_____

Congratulations! You Now Have 3 Variations of a Product or Service

STEPS TO LAUNCHING YOUR OWN BUSINESS: A BEGINNER'S GUIDE

CHAPTER 8: READY! SET! LAUNCH!

In the previous chapters we covered some of the necessary steps to take in getting you on the path to business ownership. So, now it is time to put everything into play. Hopefully, as you have been following along with this guide, you kept a business journal to jot down ideas as well as keep track of your progress. Some may still be in the beginning phase in trying to come up with product or service to sell, while others may be in their pre-launching phase. Regardless of where you are in your journey the major take-away is that you not only have a better understanding in what it takes to become a business owner, but you now have direction and guidance to help you along the way. Starting a business can be frustrating especially if you are doing it alone, but when you have the right tools and resources, it can eliminate some of that frustration.

If you are not quite feeling ready feel free to keep this guide as a reference as you keep track of your journey. Also, I encourage you to not be

VIRGINIA MARC

paralyzed by fear. Even if you make mistakes along the way, learn from them. Sometime experience is the best teacher. The goal is to get started. Every small step eventually leads to large success.

"Start where you are. Use what you have. Do what you can." -Arthur Ashe

"Start by doing what's necessary; then do what's possible; and suddenly you are doing the impossible." -Francis of Assisi

STEPS TO LAUNCHING YOUR OWN BUSINESS: A BEGINNER'S GUIDE

ABOUT THE AUTHOR

Virginia Marc is a digital marketer. A self-taught graphic designer, Virginia has spent the last three years coaching individuals on how to monetize social media while growing a profitable business. She holds a Bachelor of Science in Biology with a concentration of Chemistry. Virginia lives and works out of her home in the beautiful city of Melbourne, Florida, and her favorite things to do, when she is not writing, includes sewing swimwear, roller skating, and playing tennis.

www.ingramcontent.com/pod-product-compliance
Lightning Source LLC
Chambersburg PA
CBHW070205100426
42743CB00013B/3062